Original title:
Purpose? Maybe Tomorrow

Copyright © 2025 Creative Arts Management OÜ
All rights reserved.

Author: Benjamin Caldwell
ISBN HARDBACK: 978-1-80566-247-1
ISBN PAPERBACK: 978-1-80566-542-7

Beneath the Veil of Now

A squirrel with a plan, so grand and bright,
Hiding acorns, thinking, "I'll be set for the night!"
But winter rolls in, and cold winds blow,
Now he's just searching for a place with some dough.

He wonders aloud, in the midst of a laugh,
Why he's got more nuts than a Nutty McGaff!
While sipping on tea from a pinecone mug,
He jots down his dreams, perched snug as a bug.

The Quest for What Lies Ahead

A snail on a mission, moving with flair,
Sporting a shell, like a palace with air!
He thinks, "If I speed up, I'll surely arrive,
But why is my journey the slowest alive?"

Chasing the sunset, he hopes for the best,
In a race with a turtle, who's chilling at rest.
Each inch is a journey, each second a feat,
As the world keeps on laughing at his tiny retreat.

Hints of a Fading Star

A comet zooms past, with a wink and a tail,
"Look at me go!" it shouts, without fail.
But what's it all for, in the void of the night?
It ponders as it travels, a sight out of sight.

Through galaxies far, to the nearest sunbeam,
Perhaps all its glory is just a sweet dream.
It giggles at planets, all round and bemused,
Wondering if any of them feel abused.

Waiting for the Light of Day

A cat on the windowsill, dreaming all day,
Ponders the meaning while chasing the rays.
It stretches and yawns, in a poofy parade,
While plotting to conquer the land of the spade.

With a flick of its tail and a glance at the floor,
It ponders if chasing that red dot is more.
Will it find all the answers before it's half past?
Or just nap in the sun, the rodents aghast?

Unraveled Threads of Intent

In a world of tangled thoughts,
Socks go missing, boots forgot.
A cat named Whiskers steals my pen,
Perhaps I've lost it all again.

With coffee spills and crumbs in tow,
I chase the dreams that come and go.
An umbrella on a sunny day,
I laugh at plans that went astray.

In Search of Tomorrow's Meaning

A map of dreams, all crinkled, torn,
   I navigated through the morn.
   Found a donut, skipped a pie,
And wondered, 'Who knows how to fly?'

   With hiccups, giggles on the way,
   I pondered life as a fun ballet.
   The future's like a gooey fudge,
   Will it melt? I'll hold my grudge.

A Journey Not Yet Taken

Found my suitcase, packed with snack,
Yet forgot my shoes, what a whack!
A map with squiggles, no clear trace,
I grin and jog with peanut paste.

Bouncing on a bubble, up I go,
Chasing rabbits, oh what a show!
Questioning if I should sit still,
Or take a leap and climb the hill.

Dreams Cradled in Uncertainty

My dreams are fluffy, like a cloud,
But sometimes heavy, and quite loud.
With twirls and spins, I try to dance,
Just hope that fate gives me a chance.

In search of fun in puddles deep,
A soggy sock, I'm not a creep.
The sun may shine or rain may fall,
I'll just keep laughing through it all.

The Unwritten Symphony of Tomorrow

In the orchestra of the day, we play,
With instruments of dreams that fray.
Conductor's lost, where did he go?
We dance along, just stealing the show.

Maybe our notes are sharp or flat,
A melody made of this and that.
But laughter echoes, oh what a cheer,
We write the music as we veer.

Each funny moment, a note we create,
Playing life's song, it's never too late.
We're not Mozart, but it feels just right,
A symphony formed in morning's light.

So here we stand, our stage unplanned,
With jazz hands ready in a marching band.
Each misstep a step in this dance of fate,
An unwritten symphony that won't wait.

A Melody of Known and Unknown

The clock ticks loud, like a drum that pounds,
In a rhythm of chaos, where laughter abounds.
We hum a tune, both silly and sweet,
A waltz of the foolish on unsteady feet.

Steps that zigzag like a drunken bee,
With every wrong turn, we grin with glee.
What's on tomorrow? Who knows for sure!
We'll spin and twirl till we can't endure.

The known is comfy, like socks inside shoes,
But the unknown sways us, with its daunting hues.
We leap into laughter, tripping just right,
Guess we're all dancers in the blur of night.

So sing out loud, don't worry or fret,
Today's an adventure, haven't you met?
Pick up your fumble, and dance like a clown,
In the melody of life, there's no way to drown.

Shades of Hope in Unfamiliar Skies

Clouds above, they pucker and grin,
Wondering what wild winds we're in.
With shades of joy, we surf the air,
And laugh at life's odd, whimsical flair.

A kite goes high, then dives below,
Chasing the sun, where dreams bestow.
But what of the rain? It's likely, who knows?
We pop out umbrellas, bright, like a rose.

Colors collide in a splash of delight,
Rainbows will dance in the laughter tonight.
Each droplet tells tales of fate's crazy schemes,
While we sip our tea and plot the daydreams.

So here in the chaos, we savor the ride,
With hope as our compass, and smiles as our guide.
Whether the sun shines or storms invade,
We're here to laugh, come what may parade.

The Chronicles of Waiting Souls

In the line of life, we shuffle along,
Mumbling tunes to our own silly song.
The clock ticks slow, as if in a race,
We giggle and laugh, it's a curious place.

Patience is key, or so they say,
But we're all jesters in our own funny play.
What's taking so long? Is it tea or fate?
We pull out the snacks and decide to wait.

Conversations tumble like dominoes thrown,
Jokes ricochet off the wait-bridge grown.
We're masters of idle, philosophers too,
As time plays tricks on our funny crew.

So here we stand, with smiles aglow,
In this grand waiting room, we laugh and we flow.
For every moment spent brings stories bold,
In the chronicles of life, waiting hearts unfold.

The Quiet Strength of Hope's Embrace

In the morning, I wake with a grin,
Dreams in my pocket, let the fun begin.
Coffee in hand, a dance in my feet,
Chasing my goals in a strange little beat.

Life's a puzzle with pieces to find,
Some fit just right, others are blind.
I laugh at the silly twists of my fate,
Wandering through life with a twist of my plate.

Unwrapping the Gifts of the Unknown

A box full of quirks sits under my bed,
Filled with what-ifs dancing in my head.
I shake it and hope for a good surprise,
Maybe a unicorn, or cake in the skies?

Each day's a present, wrapped up so tight,
Sometimes it glimmers, sometimes a fright.
I tear at the ribbons with childlike delight,
Each moment's a gem, shining so bright.

Whispers of an Uncertain Dawn

The rooster crows loud, then naps on the job,
While I sip my tea and let worries blob.
The sun peeks in, all yawns and grins,
Another adventure where chaos begins.

Morning whispers secrets, a giggle or two,
As I stumble 'round looking for my shoe.
With each little slip, I laugh at my fate,
Tomorrow's a mystery I can't wait to create.

The Future's Labyrinth

One foot in front, then a twist to the left,
I'm lost in the maze, a curious theft.
A sign says "this way," but who can I trust?
My compass is broken; it's not worth the rust.

I bump into walls, make friends with the mice,
We laugh at the turns, they tell me it's nice.
The future's a riddle, a comic parade,
Each step is a chuckle in this wild charade.

Chasing Shadows of What Could Be

I once chased dreams, fell in a ditch,
Tripped on a cloud, it made me laugh,
Hopped on a breeze, thought I might fly,
But gravity's grip said 'give it a try.'

Running so fast, I lost my shoe,
Funny how plans can go askew,
The road ahead twists like a snake,
Maybe next time, I'll take a break.

The Light Beyond the Horizon

The sun peeks out, just a tease,
I squint my eyes, it's still a breeze,
Chasing rays with my shadow near,
But it runs away, what a sneaky peer.

The dawn laughs loud, full of cheer,
It knows my dreams are far from here,
With coffee in hand, I wave at the sky,
Just one more sip, I promise I'll try.

Reflections in a Glassy Sea

Looking for answers in water so clear,
My reflection winks, oh dear, oh dear!
I ask the waves, they just splash back,
   Then I realize I've lost my snack.

A seagull giggles, swoops down to play,
   While I'm debating what to say,
The tide rolls in, like a sneaky thief,
And I'm left pondering my own disbelief.

The Silent Call of Daybreak

Daybreak whispers, 'Are you awake?'
But I'm too cozy; it's tough to shake,
The alarm bell rings, a silly chime,
I hit snooze again, isn't that just prime?

Morning stretches, yawns like a cat,
Who needs a schedule? Where's the fun in that?
Chasing the day while sleep's still in tow,
I'll get started, just after one more show.

Tomorrow's Canvas Awaits

With brushes in hand, I stand in fright,
Painting my dreams in the dead of night.
Colors all mixed, a laugh in the flow,
What's that? Is it orange or just a bad show?

Each stroke a giggle, a wobble, a grin,
Hoping tomorrow, the masterpiece begins.
But today? It's a doodle, oh what a sight,
Looks like my cat tried to join in the fight.

The Fragile Thread of Intent

Each plan I weave is a delicate thread,
But oops! There it goes, tangled instead.
I meant for success, but here comes a twist,
With chores left undone, they're hard to resist.

I strut with my goals, like a peacock so vain,
Till reality shouts with a hiccup of rain.
Tomorrow I'll fix it, tomorrow I swear,
But tonight, it's just snacks and rolling in despair.

Embracing Uncertainty's Dance

I dance with my doubts in a quirky ballet,
Steps left and right, what a comical display.
Tripping on thoughts, I'm a sight to be seen,
Should I laugh or cry? It's a wild routine!

The future is fuzzy like grandma's old hat,
Yet here I am twirling, who knew I could scat?
Tomorrow's the stage for my circus so bright,
Where juggling my dreams feels just right.

Flickering Hopes of a New Day

The dawn breaks slowly, like a tortoise in flight,
With coffee in hand, I prepare for the fight.
The sun's a bright bulb that flickers and glows,
But my dreams are like socks, lost under the throws.

Yet laughter emerges in the blur of the morn,
As I trip on ambition and stumble forlorn.
Who knows what awaits in this whimsical quest?
Perhaps it's just toast with a side of jest!

Echoes of the Unattained

I woke up today with plans so grand,
Yet here I sit, with snacks in hand.
The laundry's done, but only in my dreams,
Tomorrow's far, or so it seems.

I had a vision, bright and bold,
But my couch is warm, and the world is cold.
That great escape, it starts to fade,
When snacks and naps are what I've made.

My friends, they call, and cheer me on,
But my ambition's gone until it's dawn.
A hero's journey, it can wait,
For now, I feast, and contemplate.

So let tonight be full of zest,
With pillows soft, and the world's jest.
Who needs the stars, or to redefine?
Tomorrow's light can wait—I'm fine!

The Canvas Awaits the Brush

My easel stands, all dressed in white,
A masterpiece? Just not tonight.
With brushes lined like soldiers neat,
They wait for hype, but I eat sweets.

Each color dances in a jar,
Yet here I wonder where they are.
I'll paint the night; oh wait, it's late,
Instead, I binge, and contemplate fate.

The canvas yawns, "What's your intent?"
"Hold on!" I say, "There's TV to rent!"
A splash of blue, a hint of red,
Who needs a masterpiece instead?

Tomorrow comes, and so will flair,
For now, I stick to my comfy chair.
The colors wait—they won't decay,
Tomorrow, brave! I'll find my way!

Magnet of the Yet-to-Come

I'm drawn to dreams like bees to bloom,
But all I do is nap in my room.
The fridge calls out with candy bright,
And plans take flight, but not tonight.

I stand beside a stack of goals,
Yet here I snack on pizza rolls.
The future shines, a spark, a flick,
But right now, the couch is the pick.

My vision board—what a sight to see,
Yet here I count shows on TV.
"Tomorrow's bright!" my friends exclaim,
But I'd rather take a nap, oh shame!

So let the dawn bring glimmers new,
For now, I do my tried-and-true.
In the quiet hush of night's embrace,
I'll dream of change, in my favorite place!

The Pulse of Tomorrow

The clock ticks loud, with hands that tease,
"Get up! Create!" But I just sneeze.
The world can wait with its grand designs,
For now, I dance with snack-time rhymes.

I had that feeling—great and high,
To take the leap, oh me, oh my!
But Netflix whispers, "Stay a while,"
And goals can wait, or so I smile.

Tomorrow's call sounds sweet and clear,
But here I'm lost in bubbly beer.
My phone alerts with 'urgent' tone,
Yet I just laugh—'I'm not alone!'

So let the dawn bring fresh delight,
For now, I bask in evening's light.
Tomorrow's got a million dreams,
But tonight's joy is just as it seems!

The Balance Between Now and Later

I woke up this morning, my coffee's gone cold,
My plans for today? Well, they're not very bold.
I juggle my snacks like I'm juggling my time,
Does eating pizza count as a crime?

The clock's ticking loudly, but I can't seem to care,
I'll vacuum next week, that's my great affair.
With each little sigh, I let moments drift,
But hey, tomorrow is where all the gifts!

I should write a book, I should learn to fly,
But that sounds like work, oh my, oh my!
I'll sidestep ambition like a dance in the rain,
And maybe tomorrow, I'll work out again!

In the realm of the future, my dreams all align,
With each little nap, I make them divine.
I'll wear my procrastination like a golden crown,
Then giggle about it while I'm chilling down.

Time's Riddle Unraveled

Tick-tock, tick-tock, said the quicksilver clock,
Deciding today if I should run or just walk.
A riddle of time inside my worn-out shoe,
I ponder my fate while I binge on fondue.

Life's got deadlines but I'm late for the race,
With a donut in hand and crumbs on my face.
I'll figure it out after lunch, I decree,
But first, let's check if my shows are on spree.

Should I climb a mountain or roll on the floor?
A journey to nowhere looks hard to explore.
With each faulty plan, I just giggle and sigh,
Tomorrow holds promise, or at least a pie!

In the puzzle of seconds, I play hide and seek,
Counting my giggles while I glance at the peak.
The answer's a mystery wrapped fluffily tight,
I'll drink 'til I stumble, and save it for night.

Threads of Future's Weave

I weave my ambitions on a grand old loom,
With hopes for the future, but I'm stuck in my room.
Each thread tells a story of dreams yet unfurled,
But who needs a plan when there's Netflix to whirl?

I heard tomorrow's weather will bring great acclaim,
It's sunny with laughter, or maybe just blame.
I'll craft my grand tapestry with noodles and cheese,
While the world spins in chaos, I'll do as I please.

So what if I'm late to the grand ball of fate?
I'll shimmy in style, with laughter as bait.
Life's a bizarre show, a circus so wild,
And I'm just the clown with a bright, silly smile.

In the fabric of seconds, I stitch up delight,
With colors of whimsy that shine oh so bright.
Tomorrow's just waiting for my unique flair,
But until then, I'll bask in my chair without care.

Embracing the Unknown Light

I rise to the morning with a yawn and a stretch,
As the sun peeks in, "No rush, go fetch!"
Each day is a riddle wrapped snug in surprise,
Could it be candy? Or maybe just pies?

The future is dancing, like bees on the breeze,
I'll join in the waltz, but first, let me sneeze.
I ponder my whims while I twirl and I spin,
Each laugh is a treasure, let the fun begin!

I might chase ambition or hang out with socks,
Who needs great adventures when I have a box?
Of snacks and of dreams, both savory and sweet,
Tomorrow awaits with a half-eaten treat!

Embracing the unknown is a curious quest,
With a wink and a giggle, I know I am blessed.
For laughter's the beacon that guides me each hour,
And the light that keeps shining in every flower.

Chasing Shadows of Desire

In a world where dreams collide,
I chase shadows, giggling wide.
With a map drawn on a pizza box,
I trip over my own socks.

Pursuing sparks from jars of light,
I jump and dance, what a sight!
The cat looks on, a regal sage,
As I scribble on the fridge a page.

Plans are made with cans of beans,
Thoughts parade in silly scenes.
Tomorrow comes, or so they say,
But I might just nap it away.

Chasing clouds, oh what a game,
If you find me, call my name.
A jester in a jumbled quest,
I'll laugh at fate—what a jest!

When Hopes Take Flight

My hopes are birds in silly hats,
They flit and flutter, like chaotic chats.
With paper wings and glitter glue,
They sing the songs of things to do.

A squirrel laughs at my wild cheer,
As I ponder what I hold dear.
I throw confetti at the breeze,
"Tomorrow's here! Oh wait, just tease!"

In a world of baking plans,
I mix my dreams with silly pans.
Flour flies, and doughballs roll,
Hopes take flight, a kitchen patrol!

So if you see my dreams up high,
Floating past the sandwich guy,
Grab a snack, let's share a bite,
And laugh until we lose our sight.

Tomorrow's Unwritten Pages

I hold a book of blank delight,
Its pages wait for tales tonight.
With a pen that squirts and drips,
I scribble down my goofy quips.

What's that? A plot twist on aisle three?
A penguin wearing pants and tea?
I write it down, then lose my mind,
As jellybeans become my grind.

Each page flips like a wild dance,
In ink-stained chaos, I take a chance.
Tomorrow's tales, all laugh and cheer,
But I forgot to check my gear.

So if the pages stay unwritten,
Just blame the cat—a bit of a kitten.
We'll pen our dreams with lots of flair,
And let tomorrow flow with care.

Echoes of a Dream Unfolding

In corridors of candy dreams,
Echoes bounce in sugary beams.
With gummy bears as cosmic guides,
I hop along where laughter hides.

My dreams unfold like wrinkled maps,
Where disco balls do silly claps.
We dance 'round trees made out of pie,
And watch the twinkling stars go by.

Got lost in thoughts of cake and fun,
Where silly hats ignite the sun.
Tomorrow whispers "Let's have a ball!"
But Frodo the dog might eat it all.

So let's embrace the echoes near,
Laughing loud without a fear.
With dreams so bright, we'll surely find,
Today's giggles are tomorrow's grind!

Seeds of Ambition Sown in Silence

In gardens of dreams, seeds find their place,
They giggle and wiggle, just in case.
Watered by hopes, they sprout and grow,
Whispering secrets, waiting for show.

With every sunrise, they stretch and yawn,
"Today is the day!" they cheerfully spawn.
But when the clouds roll, they grumble and pout,
"Who knew ambition could come with a drought?"

They dance with the wind, yet fear the rain,
"What if we're not ready?" they bicker in vain.
But laughter erupts as the sun breaks the gloom,
And dreams take their place in the bright garden bloom.

So here's to the seeds, with aspirations bold,
Who find joy in the journey and stories untold.
Through laughter and folly, they strive with a grin,
For every tomorrow, they're eager to begin.

The Unseen Path Awaits

Wearing mismatched shoes, I wander astray,
In search of a journey, come what may.
The map is all scribbles, it mocks and it teases,
But I'm set on this path, through giggles and breezes.

Step left, step right, hop like a frog,
Chasing ambitions through fog and through smog.
With a wink and a nod, the horizon winks back,
"Are we lost?" I chuckle, as I trip on a crack.

The compass spins wildly, just like my head,
"Direction's a choice," the wise squirrels said.
Each twist is a riddle, a joke waiting to land,
As I skip through the woods, a whimsical band.

Yet on this wild path, I stumble with flair,
A dance of confusion, with not a thought of care.
So here's to the journey, with laughs in the fray,
For the unseen can lead us, come what may.

Flickers in the Twilight

As daylight fades, and shadows draw near,
The crickets compose songs for all who can hear.
With stars as our audience, we twirl in delight,
Creating a carnival, sprightly and bright.

Each flicker of light has a story to share,
Whispered between giggles, up in the air.
"What's our next act?" cries a firefly bold,
"Let's juggle with wishes, our dreams unfold!"

With laughter as fuel, we chase after dreams,
A circus of hopes, bursting at the seams.
We stumble and fumble, yet all in good fun,
As dusk wraps its arms 'round the day that is done.

So here in the twilight, let's spark up the night,
With flickers of joy, everything feels right.
Each laugh is a lantern, glowing so sweet,
In the carnival of life, we dance on our feet.

Beyond the Veil of Time

A watch with no hands, tick-tock goes the day,
As I twirl through the ages in a whimsical way.
From knights with their armor to future cool cars,
I juggle the eras, beneath the same stars.

In the past, I was wise, with a beard full of sage,
But now I sport sneakers, sporting a digital age.
Each moment's a puzzle, a riddle divine,
What's next in this journey, beyond the veil of time?

With silly charades of history's clash,
Like Romans in togas racing back with a splash.
We laugh at the ages, their quirks never few,
As I leap through the decades, like a bouncing kangaroo.

So here's to the moments, both silly and grand,
To live in each second, a dance unplanned.
Beyond the veil of time, where fun's the main aim,
In this magical journey, we'll never be the same!

Uncharted Destinies Awaiting

In a world where socks go to hide,
Lost behind the couch, things collide.
I chase my dreams but they flee so fast,
Maybe I should just nap, and not ask!

Humpty Dumpty sat on a wall,
Wondering which way to take the fall.
With plans as scattered as my breakfast crumbs,
Maybe it's best to just hum dumb songs.

Maps with Xs that never quite land,
Whisper sweet nothings, just gripping my hand.
The harder I try, the funnier the flop,
So I'll dance my way to the next ice cream shop!

One day I'll figure out what's the deal,
With toppings on pizza—I just want to feel.
So here's my quest, a cheer and a grin,
Tomorrow, maybe—let the shenanigans begin!

The Weight of Unexpressed Wishes

In a jar I keep wishes, perhaps a few dreams,
They sit there all awkward, bursting at seams.
I fumble my words like a game of charades,
A squirrel pops out, and that's when it fades!

The cake I baked for a friend's big cheer,
Was so lopsided, it started a smear.
With frosting rivering like a fragrant stream,
I sighed and proclaimed, 'At least it's a meme!'

Wish lists floating like balloons in the sky,
I wave at them all, but they just fly by.
Tomorrow's the day! I'll fill them with flair,
Right after I figure out which shoes to wear!

Gargling my thoughts, they sound quite absurd,
A twinkle of hope shines though never heard.
But what if the jokes on the plans I've made?
I'll laugh with my cat while I take a nap laid.

Whispers of a Distant Tomorrow

Dreams that whisper like a shy little cat,
Dance around corners, they tiptoe and pat.
I chase them like mice on an endless chase,
But somehow they vanish, with nary a trace.

Coffee cups filled to the brim with despair,
I sip on the hopes that linger in air.
Each drop a promise yet to ignite,
Tomorrow, perhaps, I might get it right.

Plans scribbled in margins, lost on a page,
Life's a grand play that feels like a stage.
With actors who trip over lines in the light,
We laugh and we stumble—oh, what a sight!

So here's to the whispers that tease and beguile,
With each hopeful dream, I'll wear my best smile.
For even the mischief has magic inside,
Tomorrow's still coming, it must abide!

Threads Woven in Hesitation

Spider webs glisten when doubts come to play,
A tangled, confusing, yet beautiful fray.
I weave my plans with a chuckle or two,
But every tight stitch gives me the blues!

In the kitchen, the toast does the dance of despair,
Burned on one side—was it too much hot air?
I flip it with flair as if I had a knack,
Tomorrow, I promise, I'll take a step back!

Life's little riddles twist on a dime,
With every adventure, I'm losing my rhyme.
But laughter erupts like confetti on floors,
As I dance through the chaos and open new doors!

So here's to the doubts and the fumbles galore,
Each step a giggle, what on earth's in store?
With threads woven fine and patterns unclear,
Tomorrow's a canvas, let's give it a cheer!

Hopes Grounded in Clay

In a world where dreams are few,
I molded mine with sticky goo.
Puddles of hope, clumsy and bright,
My future plans take flight at night.

A bird just flew, it dropped a clue,
Next to my pot of slightly wet glue.
With laughter, I chase the little sparks,
As reality dances and leaves its marks.

But then comes a rain, oh what a game,
My plans are now pure mud, just the same.
Yet, I'll build again, with laughter and cheer,
Tomorrow shall see me shift into gear.

The Echo of Tomorrow's Footsteps

I heard a whisper from afar,
It sounded like a stray guitar.
Tomorrow's tune is quite a mess,
But who cares? I'll wear this dress!

A penguin waltzes down the street,
Offering me a fishy treat.
With giggles, I step, one foot, then two,
What else can happen? Just wait, it's true!

The echo of laughter fills the air,
Reminding me of the world's wild flair.
With each clumsy hop and silly turn,
Tomorrow's steps are for us to learn.

An Odyssey in the Mist

I wander through clouds that smell like cheese,
In pursuit of adventures that tease.
The roadmap's blurred, oh such a sight,
But each twist and turn feels just right.

A squirrel discusses quantum flight,
Now isn't that a curious delight?
Chasing shadows, I giggle and spin,
An odyssey of joy is about to begin.

As fog tickles my toes, I stumble and sway,
Behind me, the past shouts, "What a play!"
But with humor as my compass, I glide,
Through misty moments where dreams collide.

The Silent Yearning of Hearts

Hearts whisper secrets in the night,
Where shadows dance, tucked out of sight.
A cat gives advice from a windowsill,
While I perfect my "serious" thrill.

Laughter echoes like a far-off bell,
As I ponder on wishes, do they dwell?
With a wiggle and giggle, I craft my plight,
Tomorrow's tease hides in plain sight.

But right now, I chase a random thought,
Does a sock lose purpose once it's caught?
With every heartbeat, a chuckle's near,
Silent yearnings bloom, they are sincere.

In the Realm of Possibilities

In the land where dreams play,
A turtle sings a tune,
While owls bake pies at noon,
And giraffes strut in ballet.

The fish wear tiny hats,
As cats climb up the walls,
Squirrels throw extravagant balls,
While ducks dance on the mats.

Jellybeans rain from the sky,
With cupcakes as clouds above,
The laughter we all dream of,
Tickles the stars up high.

So let's flip our frowns around,
And prance with shoes quite silly,
For in this realm so frilly,
The future's joy is found.

Where Wishes and Whispers Meet

Behind the curtain of time,
A pogo stick takes a leap,
While sleepy clouds count sheep,
And toast dances, oh so prime.

Bubbles float with giggles bright,
As rainbows ride the breeze,
While ants have tea with bees,
In the day turned into night.

A dreamer's hat just flew away,
Chasing after a blue kite,
While kittens ponder what's right,
And elephants join the fray.

So come and twirl in this place,
Where wishes spark and collide,
Let laughter be your guide,
And find your own kind of grace.

A Tapestry of Unfolding Futures

In the fabric of the day,
Jellybeans weave their threads,
While tiny mice play chess in beds,
And hippos ballet through the hay.

The sun wears spectacles grand,
While moonbeams jump and cheer,
As stars take turns to steer,
A crazy ride made by hand.

Humpty Dumpty's on a quest,
To find his missing shoe,
Climbing trees, he counts to two,
In this whimsical jest.

So let's stitch our dreams in rhyme,
One giggle at a time,
In this wild and silly climb,
Where everything makes prime.

Beneath the Surface of the Now

Underneath the sunny ray,
A snail rides on a frog,
While fish recite a blog,
And ants form a fancy ballet.

The clouds trade hats with the sun,
As trees drop silly faces,
While socks play poker in spaces,
And jellies leap for fun.

With pudding slides and sprinkles bright,
Marshmallows float in glee,
In this world, so carefree,
The moments swirl in flight.

So grab a gnome, join the parade,
Dance with the whispers of time,
Where laughter becomes your rhyme,
In the playful dreams we've made.

Sculpting Tomorrow from Today

I woke up feeling quite inspired,
But my toast got burned, I'm tired.
The cat just knocked my coffee down,
My dreams are swirling like a clown.

I grab my mug and take a sip,
The milk's gone bad, it's quite a trip.
I laugh and think, 'what is the plan?'
Maybe just take a nap, oh man!

I scribble down a grand design,
But doodles smile back, they're divine.
A fleeting thought, a giggle spree,
Creating chaos just for me.

So here I sit, a sculptor's plight,
Crafting whimsy, day or night.
With laughter leading all the way,
Tomorrow's problems? Not today!

Sunlight Through Unseen Glass

I peek outside, the sun is bright,
But my sunglasses? Out of sight.
I squint and wobble on my street,
Just like a fish without its feet.

A neighbor waves, I wave back fast,
We both look silly, what a blast!
Caught in the glow of sunbeams free,
Like ants in a rave—come dance with me!

I slip on ice, I trip and roll,
But laughter bubbles in my soul.
I'll shine like sunlight through the glass,
Tomorrow's woes can kiss my sass!

So here I am, a wobbly star,
Finding joy in who we are.
With giggles mixed in every day,
We'll laugh our doubts and woes away!

The Embers of Unfinished Stories

I started telling tales today,
But halfway through, I lost my way.
The plot was hot like summer's sun,
But wrinkles formed, and now I'm done!

Characters danced in wild dismay,
And soon the coffee went astray.
I dropped my pencil, oh dear me!
It's like my muse just took to flee.

Those embers flicker, faint but bright,
A mystery lacking all the fright.
But mysteries make us giggle still,
So who needs closure? What a thrill!

Embrace the chaos, shine your light,
In jest we find our heart's delight.
Tomorrow's tales? Let them unwind,
In unfinished stories, joy we'll find!

Requiem for Unacted Dreams

I had a dream to bake a pie,
But flour flew and kitty cried.
The recipe? A paper boat,
My plans are sinking, oh, what a joke!

I wrote a song, my heart's delight,
But all the notes took off in flight.
They stuck to clouds, they floated free,
And left me humming off-key glee.

A funeral for dreams untold,
But wait! They dance, they still feel bold.
In jest, I'll raise a cup and cheer,
For every laugh that brings us near.

So here's to dreams that spin and sway,
Tomorrow holds a brighter play.
In all the whimsy, find your seam,
And dance with joy—spread joy and gleam!

The Promise of Unseen Tomorrows

Why do I sleep till noon today?
The future is bright, or so they say.
Perhaps I'll rise with grand plans in hand,
But first, I must find my sock in this land.

I'll chart a course with jellybeans,
And sail the seas of daydream scenes.
My map's a nap, my compass a snack,
Those unseen tomorrows can wait, that's a fact!

A dance with my cat on the kitchen floor,
He thinks he's a lion, I think I'm a bore.
Whiskers twitch in the morning light,
Unseen tomorrows feel just right.

So here's a toast to each silly sleep,
While the clock's ticking, it's laughter we reap.
Let worries drift like clouds on a stream,
For today, at least, I'll just live the dream!

Threads of Destiny Weaving Through Time

In a world where socks just disappear,
I search for meaning, giggles near.
Destinies tangled in a knitting mess,
Perhaps I'll just claim 'I look lovely in stress!'

I learned life's a game of twist and turn,
With every misstep, there's something to learn.
If thread's too tight, make a gentle pull,
Like my Auntie Edna, who likes to over-ful.

Time's like a pot of boiling tea,
It steams away while I just sip free.
Mom says for greatness I must align,
But first, let's finish this chocolate divine!

So here we are, in stitches and laughs,
Weaving our futures with half-hearted crafts.
Let's throw out the pattern, free-style away,
In this humorous fabric, we'll be okay!

The Journey Yet to Be Named

A ticket for two on the train of surprise,
Where laughter erupts and confusion will rise.
The journey awaits with snacks and loud cheers,
And perhaps a few giggles and some silly fears.

Our map is a scribble, our guide is a pet,
With a squirrel who claims he knows where we're set.
We'll follow his lead through parks filled with fun,
Just don't bring up 'work' till the day is done!

The road twists and turns like a rollercoaster ride,
Where change is a friend, and worries subside.
Each moment's a puzzle, some fit and some flop,
But we promise to laugh, even when we drop.

So onward we go, yet to write our own tale,
With mischief as fuel, and silliness to sail.
Let's name this adventure with bright, goofy flares,
For the journey is ours, and we haven't a cares!

Dreams Waiting at the Threshold

Knock, knock on dreams tucked away in the night,
They whisper and giggle, they tease what is right.
Yet here in my slippers, I'm not in a rush,
Let's brew some time, and create a great hush!

These dreams may be stubborn, they haunt like a sneeze,
Urging me forward with tickles and tease.
Yet I'll twirl in my jammies, for now, I'll just play,
Tomorrow holds promise, but who needs that today?

So bring out the ice cream, let's make a huge feast,
While the dreams at my doorstep grow into a beast.
They'll wait in the shadows, be patient, be kind,
For tonight I just giggle and dance with my mind.

So what if I trip on the edge of my dreams?
I'll laugh at the chaos, the soft morning beams.
Tomorrow can fret with its plans and its schemes,
But tonight, oh tonight, it's just sweet silly dreams!

Searching for the Unseen Path

I took a step, my shoes were old,
Looking for treasures, or so I'm told.
Behind every bush, a squirrel would dart,
Is this how the journey begins with heart?

A map was found, but upside down,
Pointing to gold in the local town.
I chased after whispers, so light and spry,
Only to find it was a pizza pie!

The compass spun like a dizzy bee,
Round and round, where's the journey key?
I'm lost on a track, it's all in my head,
But I laugh and twirl, it's not so dread.

With every step, a giggle or two,
Each path ahead, it feels brand new.
Maybe tomorrow, I'll chart the course,
Today, I'll skip with unbridled force!

Moments Held in Suspense

Waiting for mail, it won't arrive,
The clock ticks slow, where's my new thrive?
A cold cup of coffee twists on my shelf,
Am I too haunted by the ghost of myself?

Emails to check, they're empty and bare,
A stack of bills just waiting to glare.
I ponder and wonder, while standing in line,
Is this the moment? Please let it be fine!

The toast pops up, and what do I find?
An old crumb of yesterday, how kind!
So here I am, stuck in a jest,
Embracing my pause like a welcome guest.

With each tick of the clock, I smile and grin,
Life's little quirks always lead to a win.
Tomorrow may bid me excitement untold,
Tonight I'll embrace the absurd and the bold!

Quiet Whispers of Lingering Ambitions

Oh, dreams that flutter like butterflies,
Some days they tease, some days they lie.
A string of "maybes" dance in the air,
While I'm stuck wondering, does anyone care?

The laundry calls amidst my deep thoughts,
It spins and whirrs, but desire is caught.
In socks and in shirts, my goals take a dive,
Will I find them again, will they come alive?

A wink from the fridge, what could it mean?
Leftover pizza, my king and my queen.
I could chase dreams or just take a bite,
Why rush to the future? Right now feels just right!

So I'll sit and ponder, with laughter inside,
Maybe ambitions are meant for the ride.
Tomorrow can wait while I munch and laugh,
Life's silly moments are my secret path!

An Invitation to the Unknown

A knock at the door, a voice calls my name,
"Join the adventure!" it teased with no shame.
But what if the journey leads me astray?
Perhaps the couch is where I'll choose to stay!

With every step to the great unknown,
Pajamas still on, where's my shiny phone?
Excitement's a snag as I trip on the mat,
Perhaps venturing forth means more snacks and a cat!

Maps may confuse, and GPS too,
But I'm an expert at going askew.
I'll wind through the woods or stroll by the bay,
With laughs as my compass, I'll find my own way!

So here's to the journeys, both big and small,
Let's giggle and dance through it all!
Tomorrow can wait, let's savor today,
For life's finest moments are absurdly okay!

The Quest for Meaning in Still Waters

In ponds of thought, I take a dive,
The ducks just quack, saying "Be alive!"
I ponder deep, but the fish all stare,
Then flash a fin, say life's unfair.

With ripples wide, I toss a stone,
In search of sense, yet feel alone.
The lilies laugh, they float around,
They've got it figured out—I'm drowned.

Amidst the frogs, I share my plight,
They croak advice in the fading light.
But as I nod, they leap with glee,
I just want wisdom, not a splashy spree!

So here I'll sit, just me and me,
Expressing thoughts through poetry.
A quest for meaning, oh such fun,
But all I've got is this water gun.

Dancing with Ephemeral Moments

I twirl through life, a slippery dance,
With fleeting chances, I take the chance.
The clock ticks fast, those seconds flee,
   I've lost my step—oh, woe is me!

I step on toes and bump a wall,
   The cat stands up, begins to call.
He'll join my dance, all paws and meows,
   Together we swirl, take our bows.

Under the disco ball, I spin,
But what's this song? Where to begin?
The moments flash, then fade away,
Yet here I stand, still wanting to play.

So let's embrace this silly whirl,
   In every slip, life's joy unfurl.
Tomorrow's beat will come around,
But today, let's dance, lost and found!

The Road Less Traveled Calls

Two paths meet on a sunny hill,
One looks more fun, the other stands still.
So off I bound with gusto and cheer,
Dodging a squirrel that laughed near.

I trip on roots and roll in mud,
Where's the sign? Oh, what a dud!
The trees just giggle, they think it's grand,
But I'm just searching for a snack in hand.

The road less traveled leads me astray,
But here I am, come what may.
Each twist and turn, a chuckle to share,
With nature's jokes, I declare I care!

So onward I go, a wanderer free,
With every misstep, an uproarious glee.
Though lost for now, I can't help but grin,
For every wrong turn invites me in!

Seeds of Tomorrow in Today's Soil

I plant my seeds in yesterday's dirt,
Hoping for flowers, but get a shirt.
A relic from summer, all faded and torn,
What's so funny? A garden reborn!

The worms just giggle as they wiggle around,
Saying, "Hey buddy, dig deeper in ground!"
With spade in hand, I toil and sweat,
But tomorrow's blooms are still not set.

I water my hopes, then sprinkle some luck,
Only to find I've grown a muck.
Yet every sprout brings laughter anew,
Even if all I get is goo.

So here I stand, with joy in tow,
Life's little seeds, they all want to grow.
Tomorrow is bright, or so they say,
So let's embrace today—hip-hip-hooray!

Splinters of Ambition

In the fridge, my dreams collide,
With lasagna that I forgot to hide.
I chase success on a tricycle,
While slicked in mustard, I'm a spectacle.

Each goal I set is a slippery soap,
I slip and slide, but I still hope.
As I aim for the stars in my flip-flops,
I wonder if this path ever stops.

Plan A's a myth, Plan B's a joke,
I'm still here, but I'm more than smoke.
Ambition is fine with a side of cheese,
I'll get my act together—if you please.

Tomorrow's pie is a slice so sweet,
I'll chase it down with my one good feet.
Splinters of dreams, oh how they sting,
Who knew ambition could feel like a fling?

Vignettes of Celestial Dreams

Made a spaceship of old cardboard,
The galaxy's mine, I can't be ignored.
With a cola can rocket for a boost,
I'll orbit around my very own juice.

Stars up there twinkle with a smirk,
While I'm on Earth just going berserk.
I dance with the comets, as they pass by,
But gravity says, "Whoa!" with a sigh.

My telescope's broken—what a shock!
Can't see the moon, but I'll check the clock.
In my head, I'm a moonwalking champ,
While in the backyard, I'm just a damp.

Vignettes of dreams in the night's glow,
I chase after shadows, but they move slow.
Celestial visions within my grasp,
But it turns out I'm just a cheerful rasp!

Horizons Yet to Be Conquered

On the couch, I plan my next great quest,
The fridge holds my gold, it's surely the best.
Through jungles of snacks, I shall roam wide,
Wielding a fork like a knight, with pride.

A horizon calls, with chips to behold,
To conquer the couch or so I'm told.
My trusty sidekick? The cat, of course,
With his jaded gaze, he's my secret force.

Tomorrow, we'll summit that mountain of pie,
Scaling heights, oh my, oh my!
Horizons shimmer like fizzy drinks,
But I'm only here, cuddled with thoughts and winks.

Conquered beds, a battle won,
The day is young, and I'm having fun.
Snack-filled dreams, oh what delight,
Maybe next week, I'll take on the night!

Tides of Uncertain Intent

Riding waves of whims, what'll I do?
A surfboard made of Jell-O? Who knew!
Splashin' around in puddles of cheer,
With a rubber ducky, I've nothing to fear.

Tides roll in with a giggle or two,
Flippin' my flip-flops, as if brand new.
Caught in the current, I drift and float,
Imagine this action as a daring note!

The ocean's a friend, though she rolls with jest,
I'll sail on a pizza, now isn't that best?
Where am I headed? Well, who can say,
I'll follow the breadcrumbs, along the way.

Uncertain intent and jellyfish smiles,
I'm paddling forward, but it's filled with miles.
Perhaps I'll nap on this cotton-candy shore,
And dream of adventures, forever more!

A Moment Frozen in Anticipation

In the fridge, my lunch awaits,
A sandwich sad, as time dilates.
I ponder bites, I sigh and stare,
Is this delight or just despair?

Ticking clocks above my head,
With each tick, a thought I dread.
The mustard's sour, the bread is stale,
I hope it's not another fail!

Yet moments pass, I grab my phone,
In-flight text, I'm not alone.
With memes and puns, my heart takes flight,
Dare I savor each delight?

So here I stand, to snack or not,
A culinary thought, a tasty plot.
Frozen now in time's embrace,
Will lunch become my saving grace?

Unknown Journeys in Dappled Light

With a map that's upside down,
I venture forth in this small town.
Shadows dance as sunlight plays,
Will I find my way? Who says?

A puppy barks, a squirrel leaps,
Am I lost, or do I keep?
With each turn, a laugh escapes,
The journey's fun, that's what shapes!

I follow paths I've never seen,
Perhaps a park meant for a queen.
Or maybe I'll just find a store,
For chips and snacks, who could want more?

The world's a stage for my silly quest,
Maps are really just a jest.
In this maze, I'll find delight,
Each twist and turn, a chance for light.

The Dance of Dreams and Doubts

In my head, a grand ballet,
Where dreams twirl and doubts decay.
The coffee spills, I take a leap,
Will art emerge, or just a heap?

With paintbrush in my quivering hand,
I suspect my skills are rather bland.
Yet colors blend, a smudge, a swirl,
Is this a masterpiece or just a whirl?

My inner critic throws a shoe,
"Stick to daydreams!" it said with rue.
"Oh, but yet," I counter crass,
"Art unfolds, and let it pass!"

So here I twirl with glee and fright,
In the chaos of day and night.
Dance I shall with joy, no doubt,
For art's a party, don't sit out!

Horizons That Fade and Renew

At sunrise, dreams begin to sprout,
Like coffee grounds in morning clout.
I chase the dawn, a little late,
Oh well, I'll just call it fate!

The sky turns orange, clouds take flight,
I wonder what will feel just right.
Perhaps a nap or macaroons,
Oh, how I hope for afternoon!

With every wink of the sun's bright eye,
A new delight I fancifully try.
The beach, the couch, a book in tow,
Which path to take? Oh, let me know!

Yet every dusk brings laughter too,
As shadows blend into the blue.
In fading light, I'll settle down,
For sunsets charm without a frown!

The Heartbeat of Endless Horizons

I woke up today with a plan in my head,
But my coffee was cold, so I went back to bed.
My dog gave me looks, like I'm losing my grip,
While I plotted my dreams on a crumbled up chip.

The sun shone bright and the birds did a dance,
I thought 'Should I work? Or just take a chance?'.
The cat on the window just rolled her green eyes,
As I daydreamed away beneath pastry-sweet skies.

I Googled my future, it said to embrace,
So I put on my hat and joined a parade race.
But three steps in, I tripped over my laces,
And ended up laughing amidst all the faces.

In this world of chaos, who really can tell,
If today's just a jest or a grand joke to sell?
With giggles and snickering, let's dance on the shore,
Tomorrow's a mystery, but today—oh, it's more!

In Search of the Untold

An umbrella's my friend, though it hasn't stopped rain,
I venture outside, with my wild, wacky brain.
Each puddle I leap is a chance for delight,
I'll be famous for splashes by the end of this night.

In my garden of thoughts, weird plants start to grow,
Like spaghetti that wiggles and wants to say hello.
I grab my old fork and start to chase dreams,
But my mom said to stop, or so it just seems.

A squirrel with a top hat gave me quite the glare,
"Chase the stars," he declared, with a compelling flair.
So I tossed him some acorns and danced in the sun,
It's a march of the oddballs, come join in the fun!

Whatever tomorrow might plan to unfurl,
Today's just a romp in a whimsical swirl.
With laughter as treasure, my heart filled with glee,
I'll let the world's wonders just bounce off of me!

Beneath the Veil of Now

To do or not to do, that's often the call,
I put on my shoes, then I just trip and fall.
With a pie on my face and my hand in the air,
I declare that today is a carnival fair!

The fridge is a monster with leftovers galore,
But I waltz right by, craving chocolate once more.
As wisdom flows freely from sitcoms and cats,
I ponder the meaning of life with my snacks.

My plans dance around like a circus on spring,
They juggle and flip, while I just try to sing.
I'll ride on my dreams like a kid on a bike,
With laughter my compass and joy as my hike.

So let moments unfold like confetti from skies,
A riddle of nonsense, the fun never dies.
With whirls and some twirls, let's take to the stage,
Tomorrow's a riddle, I'll write on each page!

Echoes of a Path Yet to Walk

Here's to the days that are breezy and stuck,
I'll skip right along, though I've run out of luck.
With giggles and wiggles, I'll figure it out,
While the squirrels enjoy their acorn-filled shout.

A parade of lost socks dances by my front door,
Their colors quite wild, who could ask for more?
I reach for my pencil, to sketch out a plan,
But it just turns to doodles—I'm a chaotic man!

Oh, what is this journey, so strange and so round?
With each twist and turn, new fun can be found.
A tripod of fortune stands tall by my desk,
Where I'll stage my next caper in polka-dot vest.

So I'll laugh at tomorrow, it's bound to be fun,
With blunders and laughter, my day's just begun.
And when the clock chimes, let's twirl in delight,
For life's a great jest, that sparkles so bright!

The Heartbeat of a Distant Day

I woke up today with a plan in mind,
But my socks had vanished, oh how unkind.
I brewed a cup of something unknown,
And my cat judged me from her throne.

With dreams of glory, I stepped outside,
Tripped on my shoelaces, my pride can't hide.
The mailman chuckled as I lay on the grass,
"Just checking for aliens," I said with class.

Now the sun's setting, my mission a flop,
Yet laughter's the gold, and I can't stop.
I'll try again, perhaps tomorrow's light,
When the socks return, and my steps are bright.

So here's to today, full of quirks and glee,
With mishaps dancing like leaves on a spree.
The world keeps spinning, like a funny parade,
Who needs a plan when life's a charade?

Unfolding Stories of What Could Be

Post-it notes scatter, a colorful plight,
Scrawled with my dreams, but they've taken flight.
I once had a vision, clear as a bell,
But it flew out the window to join the swell.

I pondered on Monday, a genius idea,
"Create your own sandwich!" Oh dear, oh dear!
The mayo exploded, the bread did a flip,
I claimed it's art, my Picasso of a dip.

The clock ticks and tocks, as I sip on my drink,
Maybe next week I'll write down a think.
With stories to unfold, like a map with a twist,
I'll just make it up as I'm crossing off lists.

Each moment an adventure, however it flows,
With tales that sprout from the chaos that grows.
Tomorrow I'll start, with a giggle and cheer,
Who knows what harebrained scheme will appear?

An Unwalked Road of Potential

I stood at the crossroads, unsure of my way,
Wearing flip-flops, in the midst of a fray.
With paths that seem serious, I chuckle instead,
Stumbling in puddles, I dance instead.

A map in my pocket, but who needs that fate?
When you can just follow a funky green crate.
With signs pointing left, but I zig-zag along,
My GPS glitches, plays my theme song.

Upon this road less traveled, I trip once or twice,
Whirling in circles, drawing laughter so nice.
I'll gather my sparkles, my giggles, my cheer,
Who wants to walk straight? Let's spin with a leer.

Tomorrow's adventures are waiting ahead,
Full of quirky moments, and laughter instead.
So here's to the ways that life's twists have spun,
With each little stumble, we're all a bit fun.

The Horizon of What Lies Ahead

Peering at the horizon, what do I see?
A pile of laundry, and a cat that's carefree.
The future seems bright with confetti and noise,
I may be a mess, but I'm armed with my poise.

A dance on the edge of a wild, colorful dream,
While sipping my juice, I'm lost in the cream.
Clouds whisper secrets of tomorrow's delight,
Will I conquer the world? Nah, I'll just nap tonight.

In the laughter of friends, lies my grand plan,
With tickles and jokes, my favorite clan.
Tomorrow can wait, I'm on holiday bliss,
With giggles that twinkle, how could I miss?

So let the horizon stretch far and wide,
With it's curves and quirks, I'll take it in stride.
Life's silly moments are treasures untold,
And I'll chase them down while the world's growing old.

The Call of Potential

I woke up today, the sun at my feet,
Thought I was great, but then missed my seat.
With socks of odd colors, I ventured to play,
Dreams in my pocket, I might lose my way.

A cat on my shoulder, a dance in my step,
I stopped for a cookie; a fine little rep.
But sugar does funny things to my brain,
Now I'm singing in public and feeling no pain.

The world is my stage, a circus in bloom,
I juggle my thoughts, while riding a broom.
Each choice is a laugh, like a slip on a floor,
And every mishap just opens a door.

So here's to the journey, the chuckles, the cheer,
When life hands you lemons, throw one at a deer.
With giggles for fuel, I'll wriggle and dance,
For what's in tomorrow? Let's give it a chance.

Tomorrow's Canvas Yet to Be Painted

With crayons in hand, I go to design,
A masterpiece waiting, bold on the line.
But my dog steals the blue, and my cat, the red,
Now it's just stick figures, all spinning their heads.

I splash all my colors, a riotous sight,
A rainbow of chaos that sparkles just right.
My plans are a puzzle, a giggle-filled game,
With doodles that prance, oh, they're full of my fame.

Tomorrow I'd promise to try something grand,
But today, I'm just painting with pizza in hand.
With toppings as shades, it's a feast for the eye,
Now my art's both a sight and a slice of the pie.

So here's to tomorrow, a wild, crazy spree,
Where each stroke's a chuckle, and laughter's the key.
Who knows what will come, in color or rhyme?
It's a canvas of giggles, one breath at a time.

Gazing at the Farthest Star

I peered through my binoculars, aimed for the night,
But tripped on my cat in the dance of light.
A star winked at me with a glimmering tease,
I thought of my dreams, and then sneezed with a breeze.

I pondered my wishes while munching on cheese,
What if those stars hold the secrets to ease?
But instead of the cosmos, I found my lost sock,
Caught in the laundry, that mischievous block.

Each twinkle above told a story or two,
I sent them my giggles, my snacks, and my crew.
Starlight's a comedy; it sparkles and twirls,
While I, in my pajamas, try to catch curls.

So here's to the cosmos, its glamour and fun,
With laughter as stardust, we're never outdone.
Maybe I'll travel, or just sit on this chair,
For wonder is waiting, in laughter and air.

The String of Infinite Possibilities

A ball of yarn, a string pulling tight,
Thoughts twist and tangle, oh, what a sight!
Each thread a decision, or maybe a snack,
And what if I pulled, would they all come back?

I knitted ambitions, with laughter and flair,
But dropped the whole thing, it went everywhere!
My cat starts to chase it; I shout, "That's my dream!"
He just blinks back, like, "Is this what you mean?"

The knots of tomorrow are tangled with glee,
As I roll through the strings, like a dandy old bee.
But when I pull harder, oh what a surprise,
A hat pops out, and I'm covered in pies!

So let's weave our moments, with giggles and cheer,
For life's just a stitch, that's perfectly clear.
Each loop and each twist is a sparkle in time,
In this odd little dance, all our dreams can rhyme.

A Whisper in the Wind

I woke up today, lost in a haze,
Wondering where all my socks went to play.
Coffee in hand, I tried to engage,
But my cat just yawned, like it's all just a phase.

A squirrel passed by, with a mission so grand,
Collecting the nuts, his tiny hands planned.
I laughed as he danced, a true acrobat,
And thought, maybe I'll join him – when I fit in my hat.

The sun set in colors, a riot of flair,
While I stood in pajamas, too comfy to care.
The neighbor's dog barked, my uninvited muse,
"Should I write a novel, or choose shoes to lose?"

So tomorrow I'll ponder, and maybe I'll dream,
With each silly whim, as light as whipped cream.
For life's too absurd to take too sincere,
A giggle a day keeps the worries unclear.

The Echo of Unwritten Dreams

I scribbled my thoughts on a napkin so fine,
It said 'be a supahero' but seemed out of line.
"Who needs a cape when I've got this burrito?"
I laughed at myself, my own comic hero.

A dream to be rich floated up with a fart,
Like money on balloons, an absurd work of art.
I started to chase it, but tripped on my shoe,
Turning visions of grandeur to tacos and stew.

With gigs in the future, I ponder the scheme,
Should I paint with ketchup or follow my dream?
The mirror just winked, a sarcastic fellow,
And whispered, "Dare not venture too far from your bellow!"

So let's toast to tomorrow, as bright as today,
With guacamole thoughts, come what may.
For life's but a jester, a laugh in the flow,
Why take it so seriously? Enjoy the show!

When Stars Align in Quiet Nights

Underneath the stars, I plotted a plan,
It involved pizza, and perhaps a free can.
But when Saturn waved, I spilled all my cheese,
"Oops, sorry, dear cosmos, let's just grab some peas."

The moon giggled softly, its light like a prank,
As I dreamed of my voyage aboard a drift tank.
But the current was strong, and I floated for sure,
Until I got stuck in a jellyfish tour.

Comets flew by, all bright and in glee,
While I waved at a star, perched high on a tree.
"Do they know I'm here?" I pondered, so sly,
Or do they just chuckle and sigh, "Oh, that guy?"

Tomorrow is waiting for more cosmic chances,
To dance with the planets in quirky romances.
So let's lift our eyes and embrace the absurd,
For the universe giggles, not just with a word.

Dreams on the Edge of Dawn

As dawn tiptoed in, I whispered a plea,
"Can today be a circus? Please let me see!"
But my coffee machine spat, like a cranky old man,
And all of my hopes ran away with the can.

I thought of adventures, of wild, zany things,
Running with penguins or riding on swings.
But all I could do was shuffle my feet,
While a squirrel looked back, judging my beat.

The sun stretched its arms, yawning out loud,
Though I toyed with dreams, feeling slightly less proud.
Why did cupcakes not come with an instruction?
Is that why my plans seem a tad out of function?

So I'll gather my jellybeans, make plans anew,
For tomorrow awaits, with its wobbly view.
And who knows, maybe today's all a jest,
With laughter and whimsy outshining the rest.

www.ingramcontent.com/pod-product-compliance
Lightning Source LLC
Chambersburg PA
CBHW051632160426
43209CB00004B/615